guide
to the museum

PUBLICATION: *MUSEUM OF THE HOLY MONASTERY OF KYKKOS*

EDITED BY: *STYLIANOS K. PERDIKIS*

ART DIRECTOR: *GEORGE SIMONIS*

ENGLISH RENDERING: *SOFRONIS SOFRONIOU*

PHOTOGRAPHS: *RANDOMER SVETITS*

COLOUR SEPARATIONS: *R.J.A. GRAPHICS LTD*

PRINTING: *"MELISSA", PRINTING WORKS, ASPROVALTA*

ISBN 9963-580-72-6

STYLIANOS K. PERDIKIS

guide
to the museum
of the Holy Monastery of Kykkos

MUSEUM OF KYKKOS MONASTERY

NICOSIA 1998

PREFACE BY THE VERY REVEREND ABBOT OF THE MONASTERY OF KYKKOS NIKEPHOROS

The Museum of the Holy Monastery of Kykkos has followed all the formal specifications of modern museums but it is substantially different from them. It is not a museum that is completely separate from the functional space of the items it exhibits and neither in it a museum that contains exhibits only on the strength of their artistic value as are the museums of ancient Greek art. It is a museum situated inside the monastery itself and like its treasury it forms an integral part of it. Its exhibits such as icons, holy objects, woodcarvings, vestments, embroideries, manuscripts etc, are exhibited as part of the living adoration and the history of the monastery.

The Museum contains invaluable religious relics which have been collected by the zeal and piety of the monks, objects that have overcome the ravages of time, objects full of meaning and history.

The visitors who come to the Holy Monastery of Kykkos for worship and contemplation and who visit the Museum can come across the piety that inspired the exhibits and they can also get to know some of the history of the Monastery and of the Cyprus Church more generally.

Story of the Founding
of the Holy Monastery of Kykkos

*The Holy Monastery of the Virgin of Kykkos was founded around
the end of the 11th century by the Byzantine emperor Alexios I
Komnenos (1081 – 1118).*

*According to tradition a virtuous hermit, called Esaias, was
living in a cave on the mountain of Kykkos. One day, the Byzantine
governor of the island Manuel Boutoumites, who was spending the
summer at a village of Marathasa because of the heat of the season,
went into the forest to hunt. Having lost his way in the forest he met
monk Esaias and asked him to show him the way. The hermit who
was not interested in the things of this world would not answer his
questions. Boutoumites got angry at the monk's indifference and
called him names and even maltreated him. Not long after, when
the Doux returned to Nicosia, he fell ill with an incurable illness by
the name of lethargia. In his terrible condition he remembered how
inhumanly he had treated the hermit Esaias and asked God to cure
him so that he might go to ask the hermit personally for forgiveness.
And this came to pass. But God had appeared in front of the hermit
and revealed to him that the very thing that had happened had
been planned by the divine will and advised him to ask Boutoumites
to bring the icon of the Virgin, that had been painted by the Apostle
Luke, to Cyprus.*

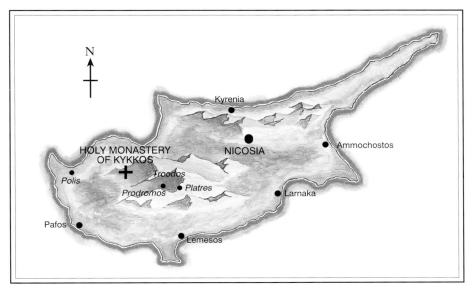

Pict. 2   A map of Cyprus.

The icon was kept in the imperial palace at Constantinople. When Boutoumites heard the hermit's wish he was taken aback because he considered such a thing impossible. Then Esaias explained to him that it was a matter of divine wish and they agreed to travel together to Constantinople for the realisation of their aim.

Time was passing and Boutoumites could not find the right opportunity to present himself in front of the emperor and ask for the icon. For this reason he provided Esaias with other icons and other necessary things and sent him back to Cyprus, at the same time placating him that he would soon see the emperor. By divine dispensation the daughter of the emperor had fallen ill with the same illness that had struck Boutoumites. The latter grasped the opportunity and went to see the emperor Alexios. He recounted to him his personal experience with the monk Esaias and assured him that his daughter would be cured if he sent to Cyprus the holy icon of the Virgin. In his desperation the emperor, seeing that he had no other option, agreed. His daughter became well instantly. The emperor, however, not wanting to be parted from the icon of the Virgin, called a first–class painter and ordered him to paint an exact copy of the icon with the aim of sending this one to Cyprus.

In the evening the Mother of God herself appears in a dream of the emperor's and tells him that her wish is for her icon to be sent to Cyprus and for the copy to be kept by the emperor. On the following day the royal boat with the icon of the Virgin departed for Cyprus where Esaias was awaiting for it. During the procession of the icon from the coast to the Troodos mountains, according to legend, the trees, participating in the welcoming ceremonies, were piously bending their trunks and branches. With patronage provided by the emperor Alexios Komnenos a church and monastery were built at Kykkos, where ihe icon of the Virgin was deposited.

According to another tradition, still preserved by the people, a bird with human voice was flying around the area singing:

Kykkou, Kykkou, Kykkos' hill
A monastery the site shall fill
A golden girl shall enter in
And never shall come out again.

The "golden girl" is, without a doubt, the icon of the Virgin while the monastery is the Holy Royal and Stavropegiac Monastery of Kykkos which has been sheltering the icon for over nine hundred years.

Pict. 3 The Holy Monastery of Kykkos. Detail from an engraving of 1778.

Pict. 4   Bee, emblem of the Abbot of Kykkos, by George Gracer.

Pict. 5   General view of Room 2.

Pict. 6   Showcase on the Virgin of Kykkos
          and the sea.

Pict. 7   General view of Room 3.

Pict. 8   View of the niche of Room 2.

Pict. 9   General view of Room 1.

Guide to the Museum
of the Monastery of Kykkos

The Abbot and the fathers of the Holy, Royal and Stavropegiac Monastery of Kykkos in their desire to contribute to the spiritual and cultural life of the people as well as to the preservation, study and exhibition of works of art, which are works of peace and civilization that were created far from the fields of battle and which the venerable Monastery of the Virgin of Kykkos has kept securely during the nine hundred years of its history, decided to establish this new temple of history, the Museum of the Holy Monastery of Kykkos.

The area of the exhibition, besides the technical specifications that it should follow, was conceived by the Abbot as a richly decorated space so as to reflect the magnificence and majesty of the Byzantine empire; to reflect also the term «royal» that is contained in the official title of the monastery and which binds it directly to the imperial palace of Constantinople from where the monastery derives its foundation and endowment since its founder was the Byzantine Emperor Alexios Komnenos (1081–1118). With these guidelines the work was entrusted to the architects J. and A. Philippou. The floors of the Museum have been covered with multi–coloured granite and marble while the roofs were covered with walnut tree wood and enriched with woodcarved decorations and gilding. Partial placing of marble with iconic and symbolic themes, stone–carvings and frescoes add to the decorative effect. The whole space of the exhibition with the various materials, the appropriate lighting, the accompaniment of soft byzantine music and of course the rare or unique exhibits most of which are made of precious materials such as gold, silver, enamel, ivory, silk, purple robes, pearls and other precious stones helps the visitor's mind to be transferred to old times and to recreate in his thought the glory and majesty of Hellenism and the Orthodox faith.

The Museum lies on the north–western side of the old building of the Monastery. The entrance to the Museum lies in the northern side of the large inner court of the Monastery. From an arched entrance which closes with an imposing four–flap door, a staircase leads the visitor to the reception hall of the Museum where, in a specially designed area on one side, lies the shop of the Museum. There, the visitor can buy various souvenirs (books, slides, cards, copies of exhibits etc.)

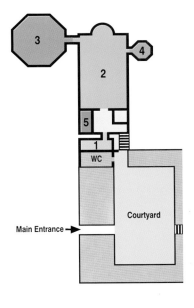

1	Antiquities
2	Early Christian, Byzantine, post-byzantine vessels, vestments, ornaments
3	Icons, frescoes, woodcarvings
4	Manuscripts, documents, books
5	Deed

Pict. 10 Complex ritualistic red–varnissed vessel. Early Copper Period III (2000–1850 B.C.) 42X20.5 cm.

Pict. 11 Animal–shaped red–varnished decanter. Middle Copper Period (1850–1550 B.C.) 19.2X19 cm

Pict. 12 Krater (mixing bowl). Cypro–archaic I (750–600 B.C.) 19X13.4 cm.

In the middle of the granite floor of the reception hall there is, in marble, a picture of a bee and round it the consonants of the name of the Abbot of Kykkos Nikephoros with the date of construction 1996 (picture 4). The bee was adopted in the 18th century as the official emblem of the Abbot of Kykkos as it symbolises industriousness and orderliness. On the left, high up on the frieze of the southern wall, lies the founder's plaque bearing the following text:

THIS HOUSE THAT YOU SEE VISITOR CALLED MUSEUM OF THE HOLY MONASTERY OF KYKKOS STATELY REPOSITORY OF OLD WORKS WAS BUILT BY ABBOT NIKEPHOROS ZEALOUS PRESENTER OF SPLENDID FINDINGS FOR THE REMEMBRANCE OF FUTURE GENERATIONS IN THE YEAR OF OUR LORD ONE THOUSAND NINE HUNDRED AND NINETY FIVE.

The entrace through the south wall leads us to Room 1 where we can find pre–christian antiquities of the wider Greek world.

The exhibits consist mostly of Cypriot ceramics from the Copper Age (c. 2300 B.C.) to Roman times (c. 50 B.C. – 330 A.D.). There are vessels of various types and uses such as a complex ritualistic red–varnished vessel of the early Copper Age bearing on top a plank–shaped human figurine framed with two bowls (picture 10). The vessel (D 247) belongs to the same period; round its edges four fully sculpted birds are affixed as well as an animal–like decanter in the form of a goat (picture 11). From the Cypro–archaic period we can distinguish a bowl and cup decorated with roses, lotus flowers and full sculpted bull's heads. A group of red–painted and black–painted vessels from the region of Attica and Graecia Magna round off the exhibition. We mention especially the bowl of the painter of "Geneva" (D 211) of the 4th century B.C., another one by the painter "De Santis" from Graecia Magna with representations of funeral offerings (picture 15), the tray from the workshop of the "painter of Baltimore" of the 4th century B.C. with a representation of Eos (Dawn) leading a four–horse chariot (picture 14) as well as the Attic black–painted amphora (picture 13) by the "painter of Antimenos" (c. 520 B.C.) with main representation that of Theseus killing the Minotaur as well as a four–horse chariot. The young hero is pictured on the side holding with his left hand the Minotaur's neck while with his right hand he gets ready to pierce his belly with his lance. The Minotaur, with a bull's head and a man's body with a tail, is pictured on the side half–kneeling and opposing Theseus. On either side two female figures, Ariadne and the Goddess Athena,

Pict.13 Attic amphora with black figures (c. 520 B.C.) 45.1X25.5 cm.

Pict.14 Tray from Graecia Magna (Apuleia), 4th century B.C. Diameter 44.5 cm.

Pict. 15 Krater from Graecia Magna (Southern Italy)
4th century B.C. Height 64.5 cm.

Pict. 16 Bronze palm holding a globe and cross,
6th–7th century, height 23 cm.

with a self–controlled expression are awaiting the result of the fight. The other side represents a four–horse carriage being steered by a charioteer.

On the northern side of the reception area lies the large rectangular Room 2 of the Museum where various objects of the byzantine and post–byzantine world are to be found. They cover the period from early Christian times (4th century A.D.) to the middle of the present century.

The early Christian collection contains mainly bronze objects, such as oil–lamps, various kinds of crosses, censers, multiple suspended oil–lamps and lamp–stands. Of special interest is a human palm holding a globe with a cross on top (picture 16). Similar kinds of hands were attached in the middle of proto–byzantine suspended oil–lamps. In the same category belongs a bronze standard or procession fan (picture 17). It consists of a flattened

17

ring with a dented external ring enclosing a christogram in the form of a cross with the Greek letter P. Among the censers we can distinguish a silver six–sided little bowl. Externally its sides are decorated with relief and carved busts of young Christ and the Virgin each flanked by two angels (pictures 18, 19). A group of early Christian ceramics from North Africa completes the whole collection. They consist of red–varnished lamps and plates decorated with impressed christograms and representations such as the sacrifice of Abraham, Daniel in the well of lions, etc.

Especially rich is the section with silver gilt objects. A variety of eclesiastical ritualistic vessels is on show such as holy drinking–cups, monstrances, small trays, lamps, special censers, chrismals, reliquaries, brooches, crosiers, ciboria, multiple candles, bowls for holy water, censers and covers of gospels which come not only from Cyprus but also from parts of Asia Minor (Smyrna, Cappadocia, Constantinople) and even from distant Russia.

In the rich collection of silver gilt covers of printed gospels, with their strong baroque style, as it had been incorporated in the art of the Orthodox East during the late Turkish occupation, we can find signed works of the Cypriot goldsmiths John and George of 1813 (picture 20) as well as Hadjioanni (S 1043) from the village of Odou (1864).

Pict. 17 Bronze standard or fan, 6th–7th century, 43X26.8 cm.

Pict. 18 Six–sided silver pan of a censer, 4th–7th century, 6.2X5X9.5 cm.

Pict. 19 Angel. Detail of picture 18.

The gospels from Russia are of a different texture and decoration; they bear multi–coloured enamel stetharia while many precious and semi–precious stones complete the decoration. Impressive as to its size and weight is the printed bilingual gospel with Greek (1799) and Slavonic (1796) text. It is a votive offering of the Cretan George Bernardakis (1804). Externally it is bound with wood planks, silver–and gold–plated, sculpted and carved, belonging to 1802 with the imprint of the Russian workshop that made it. On the main side it bears five enamel stetharia with the Resurrection of Christ and the Evangelists, embellished with semi–precious stones.

The Resurrection is encircled by twelve smaller stetharia with scenes from Christ's passion in niello workmanship. At the rear in the middle in separate relief the Ascension of Christ is represented

Pict.20 Silver gilt gospel cover with representation of the Ascension of Christ, 1813, 42X31.5 cm.

Pict.21 Silver gilt gospel cover with representation of the Descent to Hades, 1693, 35X25.5 cm.

Pict.22 Silver gilt gospel cover with stetharia of enamel and niello. Russian art, 1802, 52X36 cm.

with eleven stetharia which represent eleven dawn gospel passages on the Resurrection, also in niello (picture 22). Another cover (1737) of a bilingual Greek–slavonic gospel (1693 edition of the Metropolis of Hungaro–Wallachia) consists of two one–piece silver plates with engraved decoration in high relief and with gilded surface. A central representation depicts "the Descent to Hades" enframed by eighteen rectangular pieces which depict the passion cycle and the Resurrection (picture 21). On the rear side Saint Savvas is depicted with scenes from his life as well as the Annunciation of the Virgin. This type of cover was usual in the workshops of Transylvania from the end of the 17th century to the middle of the 18th century and especially at the workshop of Georg May II (1688–1712).

A representative number of samples of the great collection of oil–lamps that the Monastery possesses are suspended from glazed eggs of Kiutacheia. These lamps were at one time or other suspended in front of the Holy Icon of the Virgin. One lamp of the 19th century is noteworthy for its intricate decorations with gold–plating, multi-coloured stones of glassware, corals, cast heraldic lilies, doubleheaded eagles, crescents and with suspension chains made of whole angels, anthemia and cherubims (picture 23). This is an especially decoratively intricate work, typical of the combination of

Pict.23 Silver gilt suspended lamp, 19th century, 121X22 cm.

Pict.24 Wooden, book–shaped reliquary with silver gilt plates. Smyrna 1801, 35.5X25.5X8.5 cm.

Pict.25 *Wooden, book-shaped reliquary with silver gilt plates made, by Philippos Chrysochos, 32.5X25X6 cm.*

different artistic styles of the post–byzantine period (Orthodox Christianity, Western European baroque and Islam).

The Monastery of Kykkos is also famous for its rich collection of holy relics which are kept in special caskettes, mostly made of wood or silver, the reliquaries. Most of these have the shape of a closed book and they are decorated with representations of the Almsgiving Virgin of Kykkos as well as of the saints whose relics are inside the reliquaries. Inside and at the base there are silver caskettes for the relics and a cross. The silver pyramidal reliquary of 1782 which contains the venerable skull of John Potamites, a little known Cypriot saint, is most interesting (picture 26).

Another wooden reliquary of 1801 comes from Smyrna with the Virgin of Kykkos painted inside the cover. It was made by Hadjilambrinos of Smyrna (picture 24). Reliquary 5949, work and pious offering of Philippos Chrysochos which, among other things, contains the palm of St. Philippos (picture 25), comes from Cappadocia in Asia Minor.

Pict.26 *Silver gilt reliquary of the skull of Saint John Potamites, 1782, 36.5X23.3X13.4 cm.*

21

One of the noteworthy objects of the collection of church silver is the big silver cross of the Monastery, a work of the 18th century, which besides its religious themes depicts scenes from the history of the Monastery of Kykkos. In the same class belongs a silver gilt procession cross made by the goldsmith Christofis Argyrou and offered to the Monastery by the Abbot Nikephoros in 1636 (picture 30). The same craftsman made the base of a bowl for consecrating water in 1639 (picture 27), which is also an offering of Abbot Nikephoros. The stetharia of the base, besides the Virgin, Christ, John the Baptist and John Chrysostom depict the portrait of the Abbot (1636 – 1641) (picture 28).

Among the artophoria, where dried bread is kept for the Holy Communion of those about to die, we mention the silver gilt and church shaped artophorion of 1807. It is an object with strong baroque and neo–classical features enriched with corals and pearls. On the side of the enclosure the Mother of God of Kykkos, Christ at the Last Supper and the Apostles in twos approaching him are depicted (picture 31).

Pict.30 Silver gilt processional cross made by Christophes Argyrou, 1636, 70.4X34.5 cm.

Pict.31 Silver gilt artophorion, 1807, 67X31 cm.

One of the most interesting objects of this kind is part of the silver gilt cover of the palladium of the Monastery, i.e. the holy icon of the Virgin of Kykkos. A work from a Cypriot workshop, it was made in Nicosia in 1576 during the abbotship of Abbot Gregorios (1576?–1589?) by the goldsmith Toumazos. At the bottom it has an affixed, probably older, silver gilt frieze with little busts of apostles and saints (picture 32).

Pict.32 Silver gilt cover of the Holy Icon of the Virgin of Kykkos made
        by Toumazos, 1576, 74X63.3 cm.

Among items of micro–sculpture a wooden cross with a base of 1545 is of special interest. It is decorated with micro–sculptures, in some cases with representations from the Old and New Testaments carved in full and with holes. The cross is one of the most noteworthy works of its kind and it is considered to be the work of the well–known microsculptor George Laskaris (pictures 33, 34, 35).

Pict.33 Wood-carved cross with base. Probably
made by George Lascaris, 1545,
43.5X10.5 cm.

Pict.34 The Crucifixion. Detail from 33.

Pict.35 The Resurrection. Detail from 33.

Pict.36 Wooden antimensium, 1653, 42.3X61.2 cm.

Pict,37 Apostle Peter, ivory, 6th century.
Detail from 36.

Pict.38 Saint Demetrios, cameo from glassware,
12th century. Detail from 36.

27

Pict.39 Cross for consecrating holy water, 1710, 46.5X24 cm.

A rare object of its kind is the wooden antimensium (a substitude for the Holy Altar) of the Monastery (picture 36), a work of 1653 and votive offering of Archbishop Nikephoros (1641–1674). Besides the carved symbols of the Passion and of the relics that it has affixed to it there is an important ivory little plaque with a representation of Saint Peter belonging to the 6th century (picture 37) and a round red cameo with Saint Demetrios on it (12th century) (picture 38).

In the same type of micro–sculpture we can include a group of crosses for blessing and consecrating which consist of a small wood–carved nucleus held together in a metallic frame. In the middle of each side there are representations of the Crucifixion and the Birth or the Babtism of Christ flanked by other scenes from the life of Christ or the Virgin. The frame is covered with gold-threaded, speckled or spotted jewels, enamels, corals, turquoise, pearls, amber and glassware stones.

In addition angels, dragons, little domes with crescents and pigeons, lotus–shaped anthemia, roses, and tulips enrich the ornamentation. From the middle of the 18th and the whole of the 19th century the external decorative work increased so much that it mostly covers and hides the wood–carved nucleus of the cross.

The cross for the consecration of water of 1710, known as "Cross of the Mavri" (Black Woman) is more impressive both in size and ornaments. It has a wood–carved centre decorated with representations from the life of Jesus. It has a silver frame enriched with threaded, speckled and cast ornaments, enamels, pearls, corals, turquoise and stones from glassware in the Ottoman style. It was made on the instruction of the Abbot Ioannikios with donations from Konteans, Mamoneans, Balasis, Chrysanthos, Benizelos, Theocharis, Ioannes, Georgakis, Palaeologos, Demetrakis. According to tradition, during the Turkish period it was taken away from the Monastery but it was returned to it by a non–Christian black woman and since then it has been called "Cross of the Mavri" (picture 39).

The Monastery of Kykkos, in spite of the four destructions it had undergone because of fire, continues to preserve in its vestries many church vestments and other fabrics of the post–byzantine period. Representative samples from these are exhibited in the Museum.

One of the best gold–embroidered items is an epitaphios (representation of Christ's burial) of 1703 made by the famous craftswoman Despoineta from Constantinople (picture 40). The whole composition of the Funeral Lamentation is embroidered on red silk with golden and silver threads while the naked parts of the figures are depicted with slender wheat–coloured threads.

In the centre in front of the ciborium, the deposition of the body of Christ in a coffer by the Virgin, John and Joseph are depicted. At the back three myrrh–bearing women flank the Virgin and take part in the lamentation. On the right side, Nicodemus, standing, holds in his hands the vessel with the myrrh. On the sides two

full–bodied angels in priestly vestments assume a pious posture while two cherubims are near the ciborium.

The composition is well–balanced in space, almost in a geometrical arrangement, expressing with controlled movements and facial features the deep sense of sorrow that the artist wants to convey.

Underneath there is the inscription: I WAS DECORATED THROUGH A DONATION OF THE METROPOLITAN OF SYLYBRIA MONSIGNOR LEONTIOS AND HELEN AND THROUGH THE TOIL OF LADY ARGYRAIA. I WAS DEDICATED TO THE VENERABLE MONASTERY OF THE MOTHER OF GOD OF KYKKOS IN THE ISLAND OF CYPRUS IN THE YEAR OF THE LORD 1703.

Pict.40 Epitaphios (Funeral Representation), 1703, made by Despoineta, 99X82 cm.

From the orthodox land of Georgia there is a votive offering of King Heracleios II and his wife Daredjani. It is a cover of the holy icon of Kykkos, a work of 1780, decorated with embroidered representations of the Root of Iessai, the Almsgiving Virgin of Kykkos etc. At the lower end there is an embroidered bilingual votive inscription in Georgian and Greek (picture 45).

Two large show cases at the end of Room 2 exhibit the ritual vestments of various ranks of the Orthodox clergy (deacon, priest, bishop).

Coins of the Byzantine and Ottoman empires as well as byzantine and post–byzantine ornaments are exhibited separately.

A special showcase concerns the ways in which the Virgin of Kykkos protected sailors and her general connections with the sea (picture 6).

Pict.41 Epitaphios of the Virgin, 1847, made by Gregoria Costa Papa, 95.5X108 cm.

Pict.42 Stole, 1735, 146X24.2 cm.

Pict.43 Stole, 1741, 163X29.8 cm.

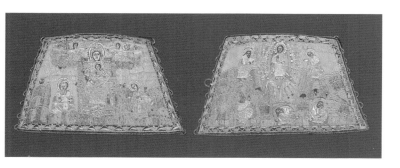

Pict.44 Pair of wrist cuffs with representations of enthroned Virgin and Christ's Transfiguration, 29X19.5X17.5 cm.

Pict.45 Cover of the Holy Icon of the Virgin of Kykkos, 1780, 121X83 cm.

Pict.46 Knee–pad with representation of Christ's Baptism, 18th century, 32.5X33 cm.

Pict.47 Golden coin of Alexios I Komnenos
(1092–1116). Diameter 3.3 cm.

Pict.48 Golden neck–lace with pearls and
amethyst, 6th–7th century.
Length 36.4 cm.

Pict.49 Pair of golden earrings, 7th century, 5X4.2 cm.

Pict.50 Golden earring, 5th–6th century, 2.2X2.5 cm.

Pict.51 Golden brooch, 11th–13th century, 1.9X6 cm.

At the end of the large room, at the apse, there is an early Christian trapeza (holy altar) while all round on special supports there are early Christian marble reliefs (probably an epistyle) decorated with a winding plant ornament and rings in which there are animals, birds and dried fruit (picture 52). At a higher level in the middle there is a large processional icon of the Mother of God Hodegetria (13th century) supported by a pole. On either side of it there are icons depicting the Apostles and part of a Large Deesis made by Paul the Hierograph (17th century)

Pict.52 Early Christian marble relief, 5th–6th century, 66.5X23 cm.

The exhibition of icons is continued in the next room through a small corridor at the end of the western wall of Room 2. This is an octagonal construction with a dome in the middle which has been painted with Christ Pantokrator by the painter Sozos Giannoudes.

The granite is ornamented in the middle with the picture of a peacock symbolising the heavenly paradise. It has been constructed with multi–coloured pieces of marble and is the work of the artist George Gracier. Besides the icons the room contains byzantine frescoes, wood–carvings and church furniture.

Most impressive among the icons are the older ones belonging to the 13th century such as the icons of Christ (E836), of the baby–holding Virgin (picture 61), of Saint John the Baptist in full figure (c. 1280) together with the donor of the icon John Moutoullas (E822) at the lower right corner and the icon of Saint Basil (E834).

From the 15th–16th century we mention the baby–holding icon of the Virgin with the inscription "MP ΘY the Kykkiotissa" (picture 55) one of the oldest with such an inscription as well as the icon of the Crucifixion of Christ together with the donor priest Kyrillos Katzouros, a work of the year 1520 (picture 54).

Pict.53 Processional Cross, 14th–15th century, 51.3X24.3 cm.

Pict.54 The Crucifixion, 1520, 89.5X60 cm.

Pict.55 Mother of God the Kykkiotissa, 15–16th century, 101.3X71.8 cm.

The icons of Christ, the Ultimate Humility (picture 56), Saint John the Theologian (E107), John the Baptist (picture 57) and the Virgin Kykkiotissa (E549) belong to the end of the 16th and the beginning of the 17th century.

The period of the Turkish rule (1571–1878) is represented with more, and mostly signed, works. We mention the icons by Paul the Hierograph of the mid–17th century. (Entrhoned Christ E313, Mother of God (picture 58, 59), Archangel Michael E213), Jesus Christ as saviour of the world (picture 66) a work by Solon Hierothytes (1641), the Holy Mandelion (picture 64) by the Thessalonikan painter Michael Apostoles and works by Michael of Cyprus and especially

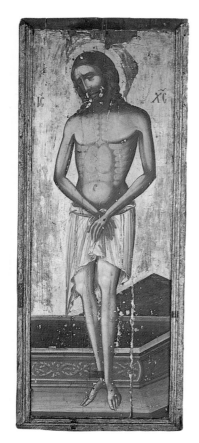

Pict.56 Utter Humility, 16th–17th century, 116.5X45.5 cm.

Pict.57 Saint John the Baptist, 16th–17th century, 95X58 cm.

Pict.58 Enthroned baby–holding Mother of God, 1650, 113.5X82 cm.

Pict.59 Archbishop of Cyprus Nikephoros (1641–1674). Detail from pict. 58.

the full–figure large icon of the Archangel Michael (picture 60) with the donor, the Abbot of Kykkos Meletios (1776–1811), at the lower right corner.

The Cretan painter John Kornaros who stayed for a long time at the Monastery of Kykkos (end of the 18th, beginning of the 19th century) and painted many icons is represented with the works Calling of the Apostles Andrew and Peter (pictures 62, 63), an icon with the hymn to the Virgin "Upon you joy" (E134), the Archangel Michael (E38), the Virgin of Kykkos (E41) of 1789 and others. The works of painters Leontios Hierodeacon (Dormition of the Virgin E708) and Gregory the Hierodeacon (Christ Pantokrator E183) and Charalambos Kykkotis, Mother of God the Kykkiotissa (picture 65) of 1757. On a separate wall, through a series of icons the evolution of the iconography of the Virgin of Kykkos from the 15th to the 19th century is exhibited.

Pict.60 Archangel Michael by Michael of Cyprus, 1782, 167X96.5 cm.

Pict.61 Mother of God Hodegetria, 13th century, 100X68 cm.

Pict.62 *Detail from picture 63.*

Pict.63 *The Calling of the Apostles Andrew and Peter, by John Kornaros, 1792, 90.2X59.5 cm.*

Pict.64 *The Holy Mandelium by Michael Apostoles, 1776, 45X39 cm.*

Two sides of the same room have been filled with frescoes which have been removed from the church of Saint Antony at Kellia in Larnaca which were difficult to preserve. They belong to the 12th and 13th century. Here we can distinguish the well–preserved and finely drawn Saint Demetrios (picture 67) who is depicted as a young, well–built soldier with all his armour and painted on a blue (cobalt) backround (13th century).

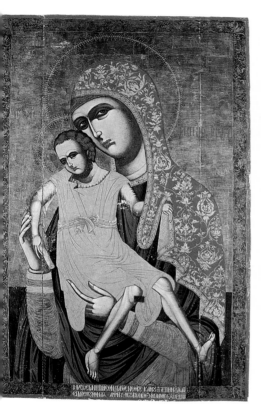

Pict.65 Mother of God the Kykkiotissa,
        by Charalambos Kykkotis, 1757,
        123X79 cm.

Pict.66 Jesus Christ as Saviour of the World
        by Solomos Hierothytes, 1641,
        122X80 cm.

Pict.67 Saint Demetrios (removed fresco),
13th century, 222X131 cm.

Pict.68 Wooden bone–ornamented throne of the Holy Icon of the Virgin of Kykkos, 1785, 300X125 cm.

Pict.69 Woodcarved ornamentation of the iconostasis, 16th century, 545X45 cm.

Pict.70 Detail from pict 69.

Wood–carved objects and church furniture items are also exhibited. From the deserted Metochion (Annexe) of the Virgin of Sinte (Paphos) are exhibited some wood–carved ornaments of the iconostasis, which belong to the 16th century, enriched with gilded locks of plants, clams, birds and animals (picture 69).

An old big wooden and bone–ornamented throne of the holy icon of Kykkos (picture 68) of arabo–islamic style, ornamented with vegetable and geometric motifs as well as Christian symbols deserves special mention. It is a work of 1785, a telling specimen of the co–existence of the two worlds, Orthodox Christianity and Islam and their mutual influence in the sphere of art.

In the fourth and last room of the Museum a small octagon with walled–in showcases, which leads to the end of the eastern wall of Room 2, objects made of parchment and paper are kept. Manuscripts, with or without miniatures, documents, books that the Monastery published occasionally, drawings on paper and seals fill this small room. One of the oldest items is a two–way (boustrophedon) written parchment manuscript roll 4.10 m. long containing the Holy Liturgy and belonging to circa the 12th century, a time at which the Monastery of the Virgin of Kykkos was founded (picture 74).

Another official patriarchal document (copy) of 1760 came from Ecumenical Patriarch Serapheim (1757–1761) and bears the signature of the Synod of the Ecumenical See as well as that of the Archbishop of Cyprus Paisios (1759–1767) and confirms the stavropegiac status of the Monastery of Kykkos, i.e., its autonomy and independence as far as its administration is concerned.

Another aspect of the artistic endeavour of the Monastery can be seen in the paper pictures and icons, engravings of religious themes, which the Monastery used to print and distribute to the faithful during the time of Turkish rule. Such pictures were also used to illustrate various publications. Of special note here is a large colour–coated copper–engraving (picture 71) which was printed in Venice in 1778 and depicts in the middle the Almsgiving Virgin of Kykkos and all round, in fifteen panels, scenes from the history of the Holy Icon and of the Monastery of Kykkos.

Pict.71 History of the Monastery of Kykkos by Michael Apostoles, 1778, 96X67 cm.

Pict.72 First page of the liturgy of Saint John Chrysostom. Illustrated manuscript, 17th–18th century.

Pict.73 Saint John Chrysostom. Illustrated manuscript, 17th–18th century.

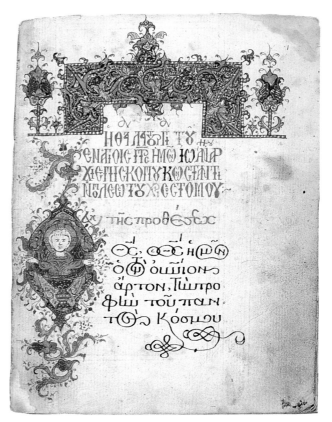

Pict.74 Parchment manuscript roll, 12th century.

Dear visitor, this is in a few words the Museum of the Holy Monastery of Kykkos, "stately repository of old works", as the Abbot of the Monastery Nikephoros conceived it. An exhibition that does not talk loudly but speaks suggestively. Old objects and works of art constitute both a national and a world heritage.

THE GUIDE TO THE MUSEUM
OF THE HOLY MONASTERY OF KYKKOS
BY STYLIANOS K. PERDIKIS, DIRECTOR OF THE MUSEUM
WAS PRINTED AT "MELISSA" PRINTING WORKS ASPROVALTA
TELEPHONE: (0397)23313, FAX: 24415, GREECE
IN MARCH 1998
IN 20,000 COPIES